C000174358

BEST
MUM
EVER

summersdale

BEST MUM EVER

Compiled by Peggy Jones

An Hachette UK Company
www.hachette.co.uk

Summersdale Publishers Ltd
Part of Octopus Publishing Group Limited
Carmelite House
50 Victoria Embankment
LONDON
EC4Y 0DZ
UK

www.summersdale.com

Printed and bound in China

ISBN: 978-1-80007-022-6

Substantial discounts on bulk quantities of Summersdale books are available to corporations, professional associations and other organizations. For details contact general enquiries: telephone: +44 (0) 1243 771107 or email: enquiries@summersdale.com.

To..

From......................................

A mother is the one who fills your heart in the first place.

Amy Tan

My mother taught me that nothing comes without persistence, focus and commitment.

Munroe Bergdorf

ALL I WANT IS TO MAKE YOU PROUD

A mother's love endures through all.

Washington Irving

I am sure that
if the mothers of
various nations
could meet,
there would be
no more wars.

E. M. Forster

At the end
of the day,
my most
important title
is still mom-
in-chief.

Michelle Obama

YOU'LL ALWAYS BE MY BEST FRIEND

A mother is
she who can take
the place of all
others but whose
place no one
else can take.

Gaspard Mermillod

My mother taught me that there are more valuable ways to achieve beauty than just through your external features.

Lupita Nyong'o

I'M SO GRATEFUL THAT YOU'RE MY MUM

A mother is not a person to lean on, but a person to make leaning unnecessary.

Dorothy Canfield Fisher

Biology is the least of what makes someone a mother.

Oprah Winfrey

If you can raise children that turn out to be people who you want to have dinner with, that's great.

Susan Sarandon

YOU ARE MY
INSPIRATION

I'm amazed at how much I feel like the greatest hero alive.

Viola Davis
on motherhood

My mother...
she is beautiful,
softened at
the edges and
tempered with a
spine of steel.

Jodi Picoult

MUMS
ARE
MAGIC

THAT IS THE GREATEST PART ABOUT ME. BEING A MOM.

Regina King

We don't have to
have answers for
our children;
we just have to
be brave enough
to trek into the
woods and ask
tough questions
with them.

Glennon Doyle

FAMILIES DON'T HAVE TO MATCH. YOU DON'T HAVE TO LOOK LIKE SOMEONE ELSE TO LOVE THEM.

Leigh Anne Tuohy

YOU TAUGHT ME WHAT LOVE REALLY IS

You keep searching for somebody as good as your mother, and that's a losing battle.

Justin Timberlake

A child's first teacher is its mother.

Peng Liyuan

YOU
LIGHT
UP EVERY
ROOM

THE MOMENT A CHILD IS BORN, THE MOTHER IS ALSO BORN.

Osho

A mother's arms are made of tenderness and children sleep soundly in them.

Victor Hugo

As a mum it's important to teach your children that they're extraordinary, powerful beings.

Thandiwe Newton

YOU'RE MY BEST CRITIC AND MY STRONGEST SUPPORTER

Acceptance, tolerance, bravery, compassion. These are the things my mom taught me.

Lady Gaga

Every baby is a
Revolution.

Yoko Ono

YOU GIVE
THE BEST
HUGS

You make it work.
You keep getting
out of bed.
Sometimes it's
just because you
know there's a
cup of coffee
downstairs.

Michelle Williams
on motherhood

When my kids become wild and unruly, I use a nice, safe playpen. When they're finished, I climb out.

Erma Bombeck

It's magic;
it's pretty
amazing.

Meghan, Duchess of Sussex,
on motherhood

YOU
TAUGHT
ME HOW
TO SPREAD
MY WINGS

It's been bittersweet
and humbling to
let her lead, and
to try not to be
perfect myself.

Amanda Peet
on her daughter

To describe my mother would be to write about a hurricane in its perfect power.

Maya Angelou

I
APPRECIATE
EVERYTHING
YOU DO
FOR ME

Our kids love us for who we are and the sacrifices we make. They get it.

Maggie Hassan

You don't have to be a biological mother to mother a child.

Gauri Sawant

I am a mother because I love being a mother.

Nicole Kidman

YOU ARE
HOME
TO ME

For me it was the most liberating thing that ever happened to me.

Toni Morrison
on becoming a mother

NO INFLUENCE IS SO POWERFUL AS THAT OF THE MOTHER.

Sarah Josepha Hale

YOU ARE A
SUPERHERO

Motherhood has a very humanizing effect. Everything gets reduced to essentials.

Meryl Streep

THE LIFE OF A MOTHER IS THE LIFE OF A CHILD: YOU ARE TWO BLOSSOMS ON A SINGLE BRANCH.

Karen Maezen Miller

My mother is
my root, my
foundation.

Michael Jordan

YOU MAKE
EVERY DAY
BETTER

When you look into your mother's eyes, you know that is the purest love you can find.

Mitch Albom

MY MOTHER NEVER ASKED ANYONE PERMISSION TO TELL HER WHAT WAS POSSIBLE.

Kamala Harris

NOTHING IS TRULY LOST UNTIL MUM CAN'T FIND IT

A mother's love for her child is like nothing else in the world.

Agatha Christie

The influence of a mother in the lives of her children is beyond calculation.

James E. Faust

Dear Mama,
Everything I am is
because of you!

Beyoncé

YOUR KINDNESS IS INFINITE

I just didn't know there was that much room in a house for that much joy!

Hoda Kotb
on becoming a mother

A mother is one
to whom you hurry
when you are
troubled.

Emily Dickinson

YOUR LOVE WILL ALWAYS BE WITH ME

The natural state of motherhood is unselfishness.

Jessica Lange

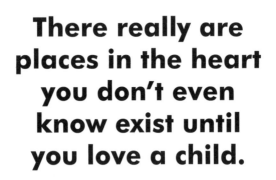

There really are places in the heart you don't even know exist until you love a child.

Anne Lamott

Most of the time you don't really know what to do. You just try to do your best.

Marian Robinson
on motherhood

NO MATTER MY AGE, I WILL ALWAYS NEED YOU

If love is sweet as a flower, then my mother is that sweet flower of love.

Stevie Wonder

I cannot forget my mother. She is my bridge.

Renita J. Weems

A MOTHER'S LOVE IS WHOLE NO MATTER HOW MANY TIMES IT IS DIVIDED

There's a lot more
to being a woman
than being a mother,
but there's a hell of
a lot more to being
a mother than most
people suspect.

Roseanne Barr

It's not about being perfect, but it's about doing your best.

Jessica Alba
on being a mother

A mother has
to think twice,
once for herself
and once for
her child.

Sophia Loren

HAS ANYONE TOLD YOU THAT YOU'RE DOING A GREAT JOB?

Motherhood is the
biggest gamble in
the world. It is the
glorious life force.
It's huge and scary
- it's an act of
infinite optimism.

Gilda Radner

IT TAKES COURAGE TO RAISE CHILDREN.

John Steinbeck

I WILL
LOVE YOU
TILL THE
END OF
TIME

MEN ARE WHAT THEIR MOTHERS MADE THEM.

Ralph Waldo Emerson

Little souls
find their way
to you whether
they're from
your womb
or someone
else's.

Sheryl Crow

There is no way to be a perfect mother, and a million ways to be a good one.

Jill Churchill

YOUR STRENGTH INSPIRES ME EVERY DAY

BEING A MOTHER IS LEARNING ABOUT STRENGTHS YOU DIDN'T KNOW YOU HAD.

Linda Wooten

Mother's love is bliss, is peace, it need not be acquired, it need not be deserved.

Erich Fromm

YOU
BRING OUT
THE BEST
IN ME

I think my
life began with
waking up and
loving my
mother's face.

George Eliot

I can imagine no
heroism greater
than motherhood.

Lance Conrad

I'm really clear about
my priority in life –
it's being a mom.

Teri Hatcher

HAPPINESS
IS SEEING
YOU SMILE

Motherhood is the greatest thing and the hardest thing.

Ricki Lake

The mother's
heart is
the child's
schoolroom.

Henry Ward Beecher

YOU ARE
SO LOVED

My mom is definitely my rock.

Alicia Keys

We are born of love;
love is our mother.

Rumi

Being a mom has made me so tired. And so happy.

Tina Fey

YOU BELIEVE IN ME, EVEN WHEN I DON'T BELIEVE IN MYSELF

**Motherhood:
all love begins
and ends there.**

Robert Browning

My mother was my role model before I even knew what that word was.

Lisa Leslie

YOU
KNOW ME
BETTER
THAN
ANYONE

Mother is a verb. It's something you do. Not just who you are.

Cheryl Lacey Donovan

A good mother is irreplaceable.

Adriana Trigiani

SO MUCH OF WHAT IS BEST IN US IS BOUND UP IN OUR LOVE OF FAMILY.

Haniel Long

MUM'S
THE WORD

There is no role in
life that is more
essential and more
eternal than that
of motherhood.

Melvin Russell Ballard Jr

WHATEVER ELSE IS UNSURE IN THIS STINKING DUNGHILL OF A WORLD A MOTHER'S LOVE IS NOT.

James Joyce

YOU ALWAYS KNOW KNOW EXACTLY WHAT TO SAY

You never know how much your parents loved you until you have a child to love.

Jennifer Hudson

My mom has always inspired me through actions more than words.

Christy Turlington

IF YOU'RE A MOM, YOU'RE A SUPERHERO. PERIOD.

Rosie Pope

I CAN'T
IMAGINE
A MUM
BETTER
THAN YOU

Nothing can really prepare you for the sheer overwhelming experience of what it means to become a mother.

Catherine,
Duchess of Cambridge

Everyone says you change completely when you become a mom, but I really feel the same, just better.

Kylie Jenner

YOU'RE MY
FAVOURITE
PERSON

In family life,
love is the oil that
eases friction, the
cement that binds
closer together
and the music that
brings harmony.

Eva Burrows

A baby is something
you carry inside you
for nine months...
and in your heart till
the day you die.

Mary Mason

They're just
teaching me every
day to be better
and I love it.

Laila Ali
on her children

YOU'RE THE WORLD'S BEST MUM

It's so wonderful and painful at the same time. I am forever trying to preserve and bottle these feelings and these moments.

Sienna Miller
on raising her daughter

No one loves them, or wants what's best for them, more than you.

Christina Aguilera
on having children

I'M SO LUCKY TO HAVE YOU!

Youth fades,
love droops;
the leaves of
friendship fall;
a mother's secret
hope outlives
them all.

Oliver Wendell Holmes Jr

In truth a family is what you make it.

Marge Kennedy

I have the utmost respect for mothers.

Chrissy Teigen

FIRST MY MOTHER, FOREVER MY FRIEND

Mothers and
their children are
in a category
all their own.
There's no bond
so strong in the
entire world.

Gail Tsukiyama

Other things may change us, but we start and end with the family.

Anthony Brandt

WELL DONE MUM – I'M AMAZING!

It takes a lot of
focus and care.
But for me,
being a mom
is always
number one.

Rachel Bilson

IT'S THE BEST ROLE OF MY LIFE.

Rosario Dawson
on motherhood

It is to decide
forever to have
your heart go
walking around
outside your body.

Elizabeth Stone
on becoming a mother

WE'RE NOT
ALWAYS
EYE TO EYE,
BUT WE'RE
ALWAYS
HEART TO
HEART

IF I COULD DO HALF AS GOOD A JOB AS MY MOM DID, I'D BE PRETTY HAPPY.

Jennifer Garner

You've given me
the only thing that
completes me: you.

Jenna Wolfe
on her children

MUM IN A
MILLION

The bond that links your true family is not one of blood, but of respect and joy in each other's life.

Richard Bach

My son… has showed
me that love, no
matter how deeply
you believe you
have experienced
that emotion, can
always go deeper.

Janet Jackson

If I'm going
to do one right
thing in my life,
I hope to be
the best mom
I can be.

Gisele Bündchen

I'M PROUD TO CALL YOU MY MUM

Family is not an important thing. It's everything.

Michael J. Fox

Fun, loving, sweet,
funny but beyond
all that, the
strongest woman
in my life.

Dua Lipa
on her mother

YOU'RE
ALWAYS
THERE
FOR ME –
**NO MATTER
WHAT**

To be a great
mother or great
parent or great
woman in this world,
you have to be a great
individual first.

Jennifer Lopez

I grew up in a
family of strong
women and I owe any
capacity I have to
understand women
to my mother.

Ryan Gosling

I love being
a mother.
It keeps me
grounded and
focused on
what life is
really about.

Taraji P. Henson

WE'RE
TWO PEAS
IN A POD

**Yes, Mother.
I can see you are
flawed. You have
not hidden it. That
is your greatest
gift to me.**

Alice Walker

I believe the choice to become a mother is the choice to become one of the greatest spiritual teachers there is.

Oprah Winfrey

OUT OF ALL THE MUMS IN THE WORLD, I'M SO GLAD THAT I GOT YOU

Becoming a mother forced me to have hope.

Nefertiti Austin

Whatever you were prepared for, none of it is how you think.

Greta Gerwig
on motherhood

Being a mother has been a masterclass in letting go. Try as we might, there's only so much we can control.

Michelle Obama

MUM:
A TITLE
JUST
ABOVE
QUEEN

We have to show ourselves and our female counterparts compassion and reality.

Serena Williams
on being a working mother

My daughter
introduced me
to myself.

Beyoncé

HOME IS
WHEREVER
MUM IS

MUM ALWAYS SAYS THE RIGHT THING. SHE ALWAYS MAKES EVERYTHING BETTER.

Sophie Kinsella

My mother told
me two things
constantly. One was
to be a lady, and
the other was to
be independent.

Ruth Bader Ginsburg

I WANT TO BE THE MOM WHO SAYS, "YES, GIRL, GO FLY. GO DO YOU, DO YOUR LIFE."

Halle Berry

EVERYTHING
I AM,
YOU HELPED
ME TO BE

Motherhood
is heart-
exploding,
blissful
hysteria.

Olivia Wilde

She was the best of all mothers, to whom, for body and soul I owe endless gratitude.

Thomas Carlyle

Have you enjoyed this book?
If so, find us on Facebook at
Summersdale Publishers, on Twitter
at @Summersdale and on Instagram
at @summersdalebooks and get in
touch. We'd love to hear from you!

www.summersdale.com